GW01182672

Original title:
Pieces of Strength

Author: Daisy Dewi
ISBN HARDBACK: 978-9916-89-918-2
ISBN PAPERBACK: 978-9916-89-919-9
ISBN EBOOK: 978-9916-89-920-5

Fragments of Faith

In quiet hours, hearts entwine,
Seeking solace, a love divine.
Whispers soft, guiding light,
In shadows cast, we find our sight.

Every prayer, a seed we sow,
In fields of grace, our spirits grow.
From brokenness, we rise anew,
In faith's embrace, we journey through.

Threads of Resilience

Woven deep in life's great loom,
Strength emerges from the gloom.
With every thread, a story spun,
Through trials faced, we are made one.

In the tapestry of time we stand,
United by faith, hand in hand.
Against the storms that life may send,
In each other's strength, we mend.

Emblems of Hope

In dawn's embrace, a promise bright,
Each heartbeat sings of future light.
Through darkest nights, our spirits soar,
In every soul, hope's fervent roar.

Like flowers bloom in barren ground,
In life's harsh trials, beauty's found.
With every step, we seek to climb,
In hope's warm gaze, we stand sublime.

Echoes of Endurance

Through valleys deep, we tread with care,
Each echo calls, a silent prayer.
In weary bones, a spark remains,
For every loss, a strength retains.

With steadfast hearts, we'll face the waves,
In every struggle, a path it paves.
For when the night seems cold and long,
Together we'll rise, forever strong.

Mandalas of Strength

In silence, strength unfolds,
A circle drawn with grace.
With every breath, we hold,
The light that lights our space.

In unity, we rise,
Each path a sacred thread.
A tapestry of skies,
Where faith and love are spread.

In trials, we find peace,
As petals weave the light.
Our worries find release,
In prayer that takes to flight.

In stillness, hearts align,
A spiral to the divine.
With courage, we entwine,
Our souls in love's design.

Rivers of Relentless Will

Flowing through the valleys,
With purpose in each wave.
A symphony of alleys,
Where hearts and souls are brave.

In currents of our choices,
We navigate the deep.
The whispers of our voices,
In faith, we learn to leap.

Through storms that shake the ground,
Our roots remain steadfast.
In battles yet unbound,
The future's clear and vast.

As shorelines shift and sway,
We carve our path anew.
With hope, we'll find the way,
In rivers of the true.

Shattered But Holy

Upon the broken shards,
A beauty intertwines.
In fragments, grace rewards,
And love forever shines.

From darkness, light shall grow,
A sacred dance begins.
In healing, pain must flow,
Rebirth where spirit wins.

In silence, whispers speak,
Of strength in every tear.
Though fragile, we are meek,
Yet strong in love, sincere.

With faith, we rise above,
The trials that entwine.
Shattered but filled with love,
In brokenness, we shine.

Fragments of Faith's Embrace

In pieces, hope is found,
A quilt of dreams in hand.
Together we are bound,
By grace that understands.

Through trials, hearts expand,
In unity, we stand.
A journey through the land,
Where love is close at hand.

In whispers of the night,
The stars begin to gleam.
In shadows, there’s a light,
That guides us through the dream.

Each fragment tells a tale,
Of faith that will not break.
In every breath, we sail,
Towards love, awake.

Temples of Tenacity

In shadows deep, we stand so strong,
Faith carved in stone, where spirits belong.
Walls whisper tales of trials we face,
Hearts melded as one, in this sacred space.

Hope rises high, like incense in air,
Through storms we weather, together we care.
Each step a prayer, each breath a vow,
In these temples built, we flourish now.

Tapestries of Belief

Woven with threads of joy and strife,
Patterns of faith, the essence of life.
In colors that dance, our spirits align,
Hand in hand, we share the divine.

Every knot a story, each fringe a dream,
Fashioned with love, in the holy beam.
Together we gather, united we weave,
In this tapestry grand, we truly believe.

Saviors in Silence

In the quiet night, wisdom unfolds,
Soft whispers of grace, a balm for our souls.
Each moment a sigh, compassion embraced,
In silence we find, the love interlaced.

With gentle hands, we mend the torn seams,
In stillness we nurture, hope's tender beams.
These saviors reside in the depths of our heart,
Guiding our journey, with a sacred art.

Lighthouses of Resolve

Amidst the waves, our beacons ignite,
Shining with purpose, through the darkest night.
Guiding the lost, with strength to repel,
In the heart of storms, where we dwell.

Their light winds through fears, like a prayer on the breeze,
Reminding us, solace resides with ease.
These lighthouses stand, enduring and bold,
In love and resolve, our stories unfold.

Beneath the Weight of Chains

Beneath the weight of heavy chains,
The spirit cries for light to break.
In shadows deep where sorrow reigns,
A whisper calls, the heart must wake.

With faith as armor, bold and bright,
We rise to fight the darkened night.
Each link a trial, yet we endure,
For love's soft touch will guide us sure.

The chains may rattle, yet we stand,
In prayerful hope, we join His hand.
For in our struggles, grace flows free,
Transforming chains to victory.

As morning breaks and shadows flee,
We stand in truth, our spirits free.
With every stride, we shed the weight,
Beneath His wings, we celebrate.

Seraphim in the Silence

In silence deep, the seraphs sing,
Their voices weave the stars above.
A melody of peace they bring,
Celestial notes of boundless love.

With wings of light that span the skies,
They whisper secrets, pure and bright.
In every heart, a song that lies,
Awakening the soul to flight.

Beneath the stars, they dance and soar,
In harmony with all that's near.
They carry dreams to heaven's door,
And cradle hopes that crystal clear.

In holy stillness, grace is found,
As seraphim in silence dwell.
In every echo, love resounds,
A sacred peace, a soothing spell.

Crones and Angels: A Journey Home

Crones and angels, hand in hand,
Together tread this sacred land.
With wisdom born of trials past,
Their paths entwined, their spirits vast.

Through twilight's glow and morning's light,
They share the tales of joy and plight.
Each lesson learned, a treasure deep,
In every sorrow, promises keep.

Through forests thick and rivers wide,
They wander forth, their hearts their guide.
With laughter soft and tears that flow,
A journey shared, their spirits grow.

Where angels sing and crones bestow
The wisdom forged in fire's glow.
In unity, they find their home,
Together lost, together roam.

The Strength to Bear the Cross

With every step, the burden weighs,
Yet in the heart, a strength we find.
Through trials fierce, through endless days,
Our faith unites, our souls aligned.

For every tear that falls like rain,
A prayer ascends, a light ignites.
In darkest hours when hope seems slain,
We grasp the cross with all our might.

The path is steep, the road is long,
Yet love's embrace will be our song.
In unity, we bear the cost,
For in our struggle, never lost.

With each new dawn, we rise again,
For in His grace, we will sustain.
The strength to bear, a gift divine,
Together strong, we walk the line.

The Alchemy of Trials

In the crucible of fire,
We find our spirits learn,
Each trial a holy teacher,
As the heart begins to turn.

Beneath the weight of sorrow,
A brighter dawn does break,
Gold in every struggle,
For the soul's own sake.

Through shadows deep and dark,
We rise with every fall,
Refining life's true essence,
Heeding the sacred call.

The path may twist and bend,
Yet faith will be our guide,
Transmuting all our pain,
In grace, we will abide.

So embrace these sacred trials,
Let wonder be your light,
For in the alchemy of life,
We find our souls take flight.

Sacred Roots of Strength

From earth, our spirits flourish,
In wisdom's quiet shade,
The roots that run so deep,
Are where our strength is made.

Each branch, a testament,
To trials faced and won,
In unity's embrace,
The flowing river run.

With hearts entwined together,
We rise, we bend, we grow,
The sacred bonds we nurture,
In love's most gentle flow.

As seasons change around us,
Through storms and sunny days,
Our roots will hold us steady,
In life's unending ways.

So cherish every moment,
The laughter and the pain,
For in this shared existence,
Our strength will always reign.

The Embrace of Community

In the tapestry of being,
Threads of lives interweave,
In every heart's warm calling,
We find the joy to believe.

Together through the struggles,
Each voice a soothing song,
In unity we gather,
Where every heart belongs.

Hands held in loving kindness,
A shelter safe and true,
With every tear and laughter,
We build a life anew.

The power of togetherness,
A fortress that won't yield,
In this embrace, we flourish,
Our hope forever sealed.

For in the arms of others,
We rise, we learn, we share,
The embrace of community,
A breath of sacred air.

Sanctified Struggles

Through valleys low and rivers wide,
Our spirits often strain,
Yet in each sacred battle,
There's purpose in the pain.

How oft we face the darkness,
With shadows looming near,
But light breaks through the cracks,
When love is held so dear.

Each struggle, a reflection,
Of growth within the soul,
In every scar a story,
As we become made whole.

With every step of hardship,
We gather strength anew,
In sanctified struggles,
A path laid out for you.

So walk this road with courage,
With faith as your own guide,
For through these sacred struggles,
We find our hearts abide.

Drawn Together in Disarray

In a world torn by shadow's hand,
Hearts collide, yet still they stand.
From chaos springs a silent song,
Ties of faith that make us strong.

Through storms that rage and skies that weep,
Promises made, in Him we keep.
In the disarray, we find our light,
Guiding each other through the night.

Voices rise in prayerful plea,
United souls, so wild and free.
Though paths may twist and bend their way,
Together still, we choose to stay.

With every trial, we lift our gaze,
Finding hope in love’s embrace.
In the heart of struggle, truth prevails,
With grace we flourish, love does not fail.

So here we stand, though torn apart,
A tapestry woven from one heart.
In disarray, our spirits soar,
Bound together forevermore.

Wings Mended by Prayer

In silence deep, where spirits dwell,
We find the hope that we cannot sell.
With every whisper, a gentle prayer,
Wings once broken, now mend with care.

Through trials faced and burdens borne,
Faith's sweet nectar, we are reborn.
As spirits rise on angel's wings,
In sacred trust, our hearts still sing.

Each tear that falls, a seed of grace,
Planted in soil, it finds its place.
With prayers the wind carries above,
We mend our souls, we weave our love.

The strength we glean from prayerful nights,
Transform our darkness into lights.
In sacred groves where silence lies,
Wings take flight, they soar the skies.

So let us tread this path with care,
For brokenness brings us to prayer.
Together held, through love's holy flare,
We rise renewed, with wings in the air.

The Embrace of the Unbroken

In the arms of love, no fractures show,
We gather strength from what we know.
In shared embrace, we learn to heal,
The unbroken heart, our sacred seal.

Through trials faced both near and far,
We find a truth within each scar.
In every shadow, light's refrain,
Reminds us all of joy and pain.

With hands entwined in quiet prayer,
We feel the warmth of love laid bare.
In every story, we find our role,
United voices echo the whole.

As we journey through the stormy night,
The unbroken kindles faith's pure light.
Together bound by grace divine,
We walk the path where souls align.

So in this place, where hearts comply,
We lift our gaze, we will not shy.
Embrace the journey, come what may,
In love's sweet arms, we'll find our way.

Fields of Grace Beyond Pain

In fields where sorrow's shadows lay,
We seek the sun to guide our way.
With every step, our spirits rise,
Finding grace 'neath open skies.

Through every struggle, each trial faced,
We gather strength, we are embraced.
In the soil of hope, we plant our dreams,
Nurturing love through healing streams.

In circles drawn of shared despair,
We find the courage to repair.
Among the flowers that bloom and sway,
Grace leads us forth to brighter days.

So take my hand, let's walk this path,
Through fields of grace, where love's the math.
In unity's glow, our hearts shall sing,
Of peace and joy that faith can bring.

Though pain may visit all the same,
We're gathered here, we share the flame.
In fields of light, we find our claim,
Together forged, forever tame.

Sacred Resilience

In the shadow of trials, we stand tall,
Faith whispers softly, answering the call.
With every tear, a lesson is found,
In brokenness, our spirits are crowned.

Hope rises fiercely like the dawn's first light,
Guiding our hearts through the darkest night.
Through storms of despair, we find our way,
In sacred resilience, we choose to stay.

The Mosaic of Divine Courage

Each fragment of struggle, a piece of the whole,
Piecing together, we mend and console.
With colors of faith, and brushstrokes of grace,
We craft a mosaic, a loving embrace.

In moments of fear, we rise to defend,
The courage within us will never bend.
Bound by the spirit, together we stand,
In the mosaic of courage, hearts hand in hand.

Threads of Grace Unwoven

Threads of grace scattered across our path,
Binding us gently, always in God's math.
Through trials unnumbered, we search for the light,
Unwoven and tangled, yet pure in our fight.

Each knot tells a story, a journey of love,
Stitched by the hands of the One up above.
In each intertwined thread, a tapestry grows,
With colors of mercy, the heart always knows.

Pillars of Light in the Dark

In the depths of despair, we seek for a spark,
Pillars of light emerge from the dark.
With flames of compassion, they guide our way,
Illuminating hope, a brighter day.

Each step that we take, a promise we make,
To honor the light, for our souls' own sake.
Together we shine, as one we ignite,
United in purpose, we stand to fight.

Lanterns of Love in Darkness

In shadows deep, your light will shine,
A beacon bright, a love divine.
Through trials faced, in faith we stand,
With lanterns raised, we hold His hand.

The night may come, the doubts may creep,
Yet in His grace, our souls shall leap.
With every step, He walks beside,
In holy arms, our hearts abide.

The whisper soft, a gentle guide,
Through tempest's roar, we will not hide.
In unity, our hearts entwined,
With love, our path is clearly lined.

So light your lantern, let it glow,
In every heart, let kindness flow.
Together, we will shine so bright,
As lanterns of love, in darkest night.

The Blessing Within the Battle

In every storm, there lies a grace,
The strength to rise, the will to face.
Through trials fierce, our spirits grow,
A blessing found in every woe.

The armor strong, our faith our shield,
In battles fought, our hearts revealed.
With courage firm, we march ahead,
In every step, by love we're led.

For in the fray, His voice we hear,
A quiet strength that casts out fear.
Embrace the fight, for we shall see,
The blessing lies in victory.

Though scars we bear, they tell a tale,
Of battles won when hope seemed frail.
So lift your head, take heart anew,
With faith as guide, there's naught we can't do.

The Cadence of a Courageous Heart

In rhythm found, our hearts do beat,
A cadence strong, a faith replete.
With every pulse, a truth we share,
In love’s embrace, we find our care.

As mountains rise, and valleys low,
In every trial, His love will flow.
With courage bold, we face the strife,
A dance of grace, the song of life.

In whispered dreams, His voice we trace,
Through darkest nights, we find our place.
With every step, love leads us on,
A symphony, till break of dawn.

So let your heart be brave and true,
In unity, we'll see it through.
For every beat, a purpose clear,
In courage found, we shed our fear.

Resurgence of the Spirit

From ashes rise, a spirit free,
Reborn in faith, a jubilee.
With every breath, a message clear,
In love's embrace, we cast out fear.

Through trials faced, our hearts refined,
In darkness dwelt, new strength we find.
The path we tread, though steep and long,
We find our voice, we sing our song.

In every fall, there’s grace bestowed,
The light within, a sacred road.
Resurgence comes with every dawn,
Reviving hope, when night is gone.

So lift your eyes, embrace the sky,
In every tear, a reason why.
The spirit thrives, it cannot quench,
With love our guide, we shall wrench.

The Tapestry of Trials

In shadows deep, our faith is sewn,
Each trial we face, a thread is grown.
With hope as our guide, we weave the night,
A tapestry bright, a canvas of light.

Through valleys low, we walk in grace,
Each step a prayer, in this holy space.
In burdens lifted, we learn to trust,
For in our struggles, we find the just.

Love binds the frayed, in heart and hand,
Through every storm, we make our stand.
With lessons learned, we rise anew,
With every trial, we’re shaped and true.

In darkest hours, the stars align,
Through every pain, His love will shine.
What seems undone, He'll work for gain,
In every tear, a sweet refrain.

So let us weave with threads of grace,
In every trial, we find our place.
For His design is rich and vast,
In the tapestry, our souls are cast.

Blessings in the Battleground

In battles fought, we find His peace,
Through weary hearts, His love won't cease.
Each bruise a badge, a mark of grace,
In every trial, He finds our place.

With swords held high, we stand as one,
In faith united, the victory's won.
No fear to face, no heart to yield,
In this great war, our hope's revealed.

Among the ruins, blessings spring,
In every loss, new songs we sing.
With eyes on Him, our guide divine,
In chaotic storms, His love will shine.

The battleground is rich with grace,
Each struggle faced, we seek His face.
Through every trial, we learn to stand,
In His embrace, we're safe and grand.

So lift your voice in joyful song,
In blessings found where we belong.
For in the fight, His hand will guide,
In every battle, He will abide.

Crowned in Bruises

In scars and bruises, beauty lies,
A crown adorned with heavenly ties.
For every wound, a story told,
In silent strength, His love unfolds.

Through trials faced, we bear the weight,
In humble hearts, we cultivate.
With every tear, redemption near,
His promise shines, dispelling fear.

Crowned in bruises, touched by grace,
In brokenness, we find our place.
With heads held high, we wear our pain,
In every loss, His love remains.

In gardens grown from ashes past,
We flourish bright, our roots hold fast.
Through whispered prayers, the Spirit moves,
In every bruise, a heart improves.

So let us gather, hand in hand,
In faith we rise, united stand.
For crowned in bruises, we shall see,
In every trial, His victory.

Whispers from the Wounded

From hearts that ache, a whisper calls,
In valleys low, His promise falls.
For every tear, a sacred sound,
In wounded souls, His love is found.

Where burdens weigh and shadows loom,
He brings us hope, dispelling gloom.
In quiet moments, He draws us near,
With gentle grace, He calms our fear.

Through every wound, His light will shine,
In brokenness, our hearts align.
With open hands, we seek His face,
In whispered prayers, we find our place.

The wounded cry, a song of grace,
In love’s embrace, we find our space.
Through every scar, a story flows,
In whispered truths, our spirit grows.

So listen close, the wounded sing,
A melody of hope they bring.
In seeking Him, we rise anew,
In every whisper, He speaks true.

Wings of Courage in Adversity

In shadows deep, our spirits soar,
With faith as light, we seek the door.
Through trials fierce and storms that rage,
We find our strength, the heart's true sage.

For every wound that time reveals,
A deeper truth, our spirit heals.
With courage found in darkest night,
We rise again, prepared to fight.

In struggles met, we find our grace,
In every fear, we find our place.
The wings of hope, though worn and frayed,
Lift us anew, where love’s displayed.

So let us stand, united strong,
In whispered prayers, our souls belong.
For when we trust, we are set free,
In faith's embrace, we truly see.

The Garden Where We Weep

In quiet corners, sorrow blooms,
Where heartfelt cries dispel the glooms.
Each tear a seed, each ache a prayer,
In this garden, love meets despair.

Among the thorns, our spirits strive,
With gentle grace, we learn to thrive.
The petals soft, a tender touch,
Remind us that we’re not alone much.

As seasons change, so do our pains,
In winter's chill, our hope remains.
For in this soil of grief and loss,
We find the strength to bear the cross.

And from the depths of sorrow’s night,
A dawn will break, a guiding light.
The garden where we weep may grow,
A testament, our hearts will show.

Harmony from Heartache

From brokenness, a song may rise,
In heartache's tune, the spirit flies.
With every note, we stitch the seams,
Creating harmony from shattered dreams.

Through trials faced and battles lost,
We learn anew the heavy cost.
Yet in the silence, wisdom waits,
With open arms, our heart creates.

Each sorrow shared, a bridge we build,
In love's embrace, our wounds are healed.
For every tear that falls in pain,
A melody of hope remains.

In unity, our voices blend,
Transforming heartache, we ascend.
With faith as guide, we dance through strife,
In harmony, we find our life.

Light Through the Cracks

In broken vessels, light pours through,
A glimpse of grace in all we do.
Through shattered dreams, the beams will shine,
Reminders that our hearts entwine.

Emerging from the darkest plight,
The soul ignites with borrowed light.
With every crack, a story speaks,
Of strength unveiled, of light that seeks.

In moments fraught with doubt and fear,
We feel the presence, ever near.
In glimmers faint, our hopes arise,
Through trials met, the spirit flies.

Let us embrace the broken parts,
For through the cracks, the light imparts.
In unity, our shadows dance,
As hope ignites a second chance.

Seeds of Transformation

In the quiet earth, hope is sown,
Each tiny seed whispers of growth.
With faith and light, their roots are grown,
From darkness, creation's sweet oath.

Nurtured by rain and sun's embrace,
They stretch and yearn toward the sky.
In every struggle, there's grace,
Transformed life, as shadows pass by.

The beauty of change is profound,
As blossoms burst forth, hearts ignite.
A garden of blessings surrounds,
Each petal, a testament bright.

In patience, the seasons will turn,
As spirits renew with each dawn.
Desires of the heart, they will burn,
For in love, all fears are withdrawn.

So plant in your soul, dreams divine,
Let light and truth guide your way.
For in every heart, hope will shine,
And seeds of transformation will stay.

Stories Etched in Time

In ages past, the tales were spun,
By fireside warmth and whispered prayer.
Legends woven, the old and young,
In heart and mind, they linger there.

Pages turned by hands so kind,
Each story a journey, a quest.
Through trials faced, wisdom we find,
In love and courage, we are blessed.

The echoes of laughter and tears,
In chapters of life, forever remain.
Moments of joy, and even of fears,
Etched in our hearts, like a sacred chain.

We gather these stories, like seeds of grace,
To pass down the wisdom we've learned.
In every heart, there's a sacred space,
Where the fires of the past are burned.

So listen closely, dear soul, to the tales,
For in them the truth of our journey lies.
Each heartbeat a rhythm, each breath never pales,
In stories etched, our spirit flies.

Harbors Amidst the Tempest

In storms that rage and winds that howl,
When waves crash loud and shadows loom,
We seek the shore, we hear the call,
A harbor's grace amidst the gloom.

Within our hearts, there lies a light,
A promise of peace, a guiding star.
Through darkest nights, we hold on tight,
For hope will carry us near and far.

So cast your fears on winds that blow,
Embrace the calm that follows strife.
In unity, our spirits grow,
Together bound, we rise in life.

Though tempests may shake the steadfast ground,
Our faith remains anchored, strong and true.
In shared existence, love is found,
Through harbors of grace, we break anew.

With every struggle, we find our way,
Through turbulent waters, our hearts align.
For in life's storms, we'll find the day,
Harbors amidst the tempest, divine.

Blessings in the Struggle

In trials faced, we seek the light,
Each struggle a lesson, each burden a guide.
With courage, we rise, ready to fight,
For in every shadow, our spirits confide.

Every tear shed is a seed of grace,
Transforming our hearts, making us whole.
In brokenness, we find our place,
A tapestry woven in spirit and soul.

Count not the troubles, but the gifts they bring,
For in every hardship, there's beauty to find.
With faith as our anchor, our voices will sing,
In the blessings of struggle, we grow intertwined.

So hold on, dear soul, through trials you face,
For love's gentle hand is guiding your way.
In the depths of despair, we'll find our grace,
In blessings bestowed, we rise each new day.

Let gratitude flourish in shadows of night,
For each step we take is a step to the dawn.
In the blessings of struggle, we find our light,
With hearts intertwined, we're forever reborn.

The Altar of Broken Dreams

Upon the altar, dreams lay bare,
Whispers of hope fill the air.
Crumpled wishes, lost in time,
Yet in the shadows, love will climb.

Tears are offered, a sacred rite,
In the stillness, souls take flight.
Each fragment shines, a guiding star,
Leading the weary from afar.

In fragments gathered, grace is found,
Broken paths, with mercy crowned.
Trust in the journey, step by step,
For from the ruins, dreams are kept.

A heart once shattered, now made whole,
Touched by the fire, refined the soul.
On this altar, burdens cease,
As broken dreams sing songs of peace.

Harmony in Dissonance

In the chaos, a gentle song,
Notes in discord, yet they belong.
Voices rise from depths of strife,
A symphony of rugged life.

Through grief and loss, the heart will mend,
Dissonance leads to joy, my friend.
In shadows deep, light finds a way,
Embracing night, we greet the day.

Every struggle, a note to play,
Each heartbeat guides the hopeful sway.
Together woven, we learn to dance,
In disarray, we find our chance.

So let the discord echo wide,
For in our hearts, God will abide.
From every trial, our spirits rise,
Creating harmony in the skies.

Souls Refined by Fire

Through trials fierce, we forge our fate,
In blazing flames, we contemplate.
A spirit tempered by the heat,
Emerging strong, no hint of defeat.

In every ember, wisdom grows,
The heart ignites, as passion flows.
From ashes cast, new life will bloom,
In the fire's glow, dispelling gloom.

Each struggle faced, a lesson learned,
In the furnace, our hearts have burned.
When shadows call, we stand and fight,
For in the dark, we find our light.

Souls refined, like gold so pure,
In unity, we shall endure.
With faith in hand, we march as one,
Through trials faced, our victory's won.

Echoes of the Redeemed

In quiet moments, voices ring,
Echoes of hope, our hearts take wing.
A melody of love divine,
In every tear, the stars align.

From shadows deep, redemption calls,
Upon our knees, we rise, not fall.
Each whisper tells of battles won,
In every struggle, the race is run.

In sacred spaces, spirits soar,
Echoes of grace, forevermore.
Hands lifted high, in joy we sing,
For in the night, new songs take wing.

Through every sorrow, voices blend,
In unity, we find our end.
The echoes linger, sweet and clear,
Reminders of love, held so dear.

A Soul's Testament Through Pain

In shadows deep where sorrows dwell,
I wander forth, my heart a shell.
Yet in this ache, a whisper calls,
'Tis through the pain, true spirit sprawls.

Each tear I've shed, a sacred gift,
In trials fierce, my soul will lift.
For every wound, an ember glows,
In darkest nights, the light still grows.

With every breath, I seek the grace,
Transcending tremors, I find my place.
For in the suffering, spirits bloom,
A testament forged from the gloom.

The scars I wear tell stories grand,
Of battles fought, of hope unplanned.
This heart of mine, though torn and frail,
Is filled with love, a holy trail.

So let the storms of life arise,
For in the tempest, faith defies.
My soul shall rise, adorned in light,
A shining truth in endless night.

The Masterpiece of the Torn

Shattered dreams lie at my feet,
Yet beauty grows where sorrows meet.
In fragments lost, I find my song,
A masterpiece where I belong.

With every break, a chance to mend,
The brokenness will not offend.
For in the cracks, new visions gleam,
Each tear a part of life’s grand dream.

The artist’s hand shapes pain to art,
A canvas painted with the heart.
From chaos blooms a vibrant hue,
In darkest hours, the light breaks through.

Resilience sings, a sweet refrain,
In every loss, I find the gain.
Through bruised and battered, I arise,
A testament to love that ties.

In every struggle, grace abounds,
The sacred echoes, life resounds.
From ashes rise, a spirit reborn,
In love's embrace, I'm never torn.

So let the storms rage all around,
In every heartbeat, hope is found.
Each trial faced, my soul refined,
The masterpiece of the torn, aligned.

Heartstrings of Heavenly Harmony

In every note, a prayer takes flight,
A melody born from love's own light.
With heartstrings pulled by grace divine,
I find my peace in love's design.

The symphony of souls entwined,
In notes of joy, the lost we find.
Each harmony, a sacred bond,
Together we rise, our spirits fond.

Through trials faced, our voices blend,
In unity, we learn to mend.
The rhythm of life, a sacred beat,
In every heart, we feel the heat.

So let the chords of faith resound,
In every silence, love is found.
With every breath, the song perseveres,
A chorus sung throughout the years.

In every tear, a note rings true,
A celebration of me and you.
With open hearts, let us proclaim,
The heartstrings of our love's acclaim.

In heavenly harmony we unite,
Each voice a beacon, purest light.
In this divine embrace we thrive,
For love, sweet love, keeps hope alive.

Fountains of Inner Light

In the depths of the soul, we find
Fountains of love, pure and kind.
Each drop, a whisper of grace,
Illuminating the darkest place.

Rays of wisdom, soft and bright,
Guide our steps, dispelling night.
With every breath, a sacred song,
Leading us where we belong.

Faith flows freely, like a stream,
Nourishing hopes, igniting dream.
In silence, we hear the call,
To rise together, never fall.

Hearts ablaze with boundless fire,
Awakening our true desire.
In unity, we take our stand,
Fountains of light, hand in hand.

Let us cherish this divine art,
As we share love, heart to heart.
In the realm of the spirit's flight,
We drink deep from the inner light.

Echoing Hearts of Purpose

In the stillness, a voice is heard,
Echoing loud without a word.
Hearts aligned in rhythmic grace,
Together we find our sacred place.

Each pulse, a prayer sent high,
Guiding the lost as they try.
Bound by purpose, we ignite,
A flame that brings forth endless light.

With patience, we tend the flame,
Carrying forth our sacred name.
In collective strength, we thrive,
Echoing hearts, ever alive.

Through trials, we rise and soar,
Finding joy in opening doors.
In the tapestry of divine weave,
We discover the strength to believe.

As stars align, we find our way,
In purpose deep, we choose to stay.
Together, we journey, side by side,
In echoing hearts, we take our pride.

Wings of the Spirit

Lifted high by unseen wings,
The spirit dances, freedom sings.
In the breeze, we feel the lift,
A precious, gentle, sacred gift.

Every heartbeat, a flight of grace,
Taking us to a holy place.
With trust, we soar, embracing the sky,
Wings of the spirit, we learn to fly.

Through trials, our wings grow strong,
Resilient, we hum our song.
In unity, we break each chain,
Finding joy in the sacred gain.

Whispers of love call us near,
In every moment, the path is clear.
Together, we reach for the divine,
Wings of the spirit, our hearts align.

So let us rise, fearless and free,
Embracing the love that calls to thee.
In the depths of our sacred flight,
We find our peace, our endless light.

Shields of Celestial Armor

In the battle of light and dark,
We find our strength, ignite the spark.
Wielding love like a mighty sword,
We stand united, praised the Lord.

Shields of faith, we raise them high,
Defending truth as time goes by.
In solidarity, hearts entwined,
We seek the peace our souls must find.

With every challenge that comes our way,
In prayer and hope, we are led to stay.
Armored by grace, we face the test,
In the arms of love, we find our rest.

Together we march, hand in hand,
Through trials and storms, we take our stand.
The armor shines, a radiant light,
Guiding us through the dark of night.

In the embrace of celestial grace,
We find our strength in every place.
For love's true power will never fade,
Our shields will hold, our hearts displayed.

Melodies from the Fractured Soul

In silence whispers grace's call,
A heart once shattered stands up tall.
Each note a prayer, soft yet bold,
Resonates through stories told.

In darkness found, a flicker gleams,
Awakening the lost, their dreams.
With every chord, the spirit soars,
Through brokenness, the music pours.

Embrace the wounds, let healing flow,
Each melody a way to grow.
With faith entwined, we rise anew,
A song of hope breaks through the blue.

Amidst the trials, voices blend,
A symphony that will not end.
Together we lift our souls in song,
In unity, we all belong.

So let the fractured find the whole,
In every beat, a whispered goal.
Transforming pain to sweet refrain,
In melodies, no love is vain.

Rising from the Rubble

From ashes deep, we find our way,
With faith as light, we greet the day.
The rubble speaks of lessons learned,
In every heart, a fire burned.

With strength reborn, our spirits climb,
Against the odds, we bridge the time.
Each step we take, a testament,
In every struggle, a sacred event.

Hope is the anchor in the storm,
With every trial, we are reborn.
The shadows flee before the dawn,
In unity, we're never gone.

Together, hand in hand we stand,
Constructing dreams upon this land.
From every piece, we build a throne,
In rising strong, we've found our home.

The past may haunt, but we shall fight,
With love as shield, we seek the light.
From rubble high, a spirit free,
In rising hope, we claim our plea.

The Rainbow After Ashes

In shadows cast by loss's hand,
A promise blooms across the land.
After the storm, the skies are clear,
A vibrant arc, we hold it dear.

Each color speaks of trials faced,
With every hue, a love embraced.
In laughter's joy and sorrow's song,
The rainbow shows that we belong.

Though ashes fall and skies are gray,
We turn to hope, to light our way.
A spectrum bright, it paints the soul,
In every heart, it finds its role.

The beauty springs from pain and fear,
With every drop, a voice we hear.
In unity, we claim our place,
With open arms and loving grace.

So let us stand in rain's embrace,
For every tear, there's shining space.
In every storm, the promise spreads,
A rainbow forms where love now treads.

Love's Unbreakable Bond

In quiet moments, hearts entwine,
A sacred link, a love divine.
Through trials faced and storms that rage,
An endless tale on every page.

No distance masks this sacred tie,
In every breath, we reply.
With eyes that see beyond the veil,
In every whisper, love prevails.

The world may shift, but we remain,
Through joy and tears, through loss and gain.
In every heartbeat, truth resounds,
In gently woven, faith abounds.

So let us cherish what we've found,
In every moment, love unbound.
For in this bond, we rise and fall,
In love’s embrace, we conquer all.

Together, through the light and dark,
Each spark ignites our inner arc.
In unity, our spirits soar,
In love’s embrace, forevermore.

Shadows of Joy in Despair

In the valley where sorrow walks low,
Whispers of hope like wind gently blow.
In darkness, a spark ignites the soul,
The heart finds strength, reaches its goal.

A flicker of light in the deepest night,
Guiding the lost, turning wrongs into right.
With faith as a lantern, we find our way,
Unfolding the promise of a brighter day.

Through trials of life, our spirits must climb,
Finding sweet comfort in love's gentle rhyme.
In shadows of joy, despair fades away,
Caressed by the dawn, as night turns to day.

Embracing the journey, we learn to forgive,
In unity's strength, together we live.
In shadows, we gather, our burdens we share,
Transforming our sorrow, whispering a prayer.

So let not despair steal the joy from your heart,
For in every shadow, a miracle can start.
In the fabric of sorrow, joy we will weave,
Finding a pathway through which we believe.

Echoing Through the Abyss

In the depths of the silence, a voice breaks the night,
Calling forth brave souls to awaken their light.
Each echo a whisper from heavens above,
Reminding the weary of reason and love.

When shadows envelop and chaos takes hold,
The spirit's resolve becomes fierce and bold.
Through valleys of trials, the heart learns to sing,
As faith's gentle bell tolls, awakening spring.

The abyss may be heavy, its grip may be tough,
But faith is the beacon, and love is enough.
In darkness, the echoes resound with sweet grace,
Guiding all wanderers to a sacred place.

Like waves crashing softly on shores made of stone,
Resilience shines bright, in the night we are shown.
For deep in the abyss, the soul finds its fire,
Awakening dreams to climb ever higher.

So listen to echoes, let their wisdom be found,
Transforming the silence with love all around.
In the heart of the abyss, hope’s song will arise,
In the dance of the shadows, we reach for the skies.

Flowing Rivers in Dry Lands

In barren landscapes where hopes seem to dry,
Awakens the promise of rain from the sky.
Like flowing rivers that dance on the earth,
A reminder of life and the beauty of birth.

The cracked soil does yearn for the touch of the rain,
Each droplet a blessing to quench every pain.
From desert to meadow, the spirit is free,
Transforming the barren to lush tapestry.

Through trials we wander in search of the stream,
In shadows of doubt, we find light in our dream.
The rivers of kindness flow deep in the heart,
Binding us gently, never to part.

In the stillness of night, let hope be our guide,
For flowing rivers will turn with the tide.
In prayerful reflection, we stand hand in hand,
In unity flowing through this sacred land.

With arms open wide, let the waters embrace,
Healing the broken with mercy and grace.
In flowing rivers, we journey as one,
Finding our solace under the sun.

The Forged Forge of Belief

In the furnace of trials, our spirits are shaped,
With each fiery breath, our destinies draped.
Forged in the lessons of faith and of trust,
Iron becomes gold, as hope turns to dust.

Through hammers of challenge, resilience we gain,
In the crucible's heat, we rise through the pain.
The forge of belief, where the heart learns to sing,
Crafting our futures, while the angels take wing.

With every strike echoing deep in the night,
We're sculpted by love, in the shadows, the light.
Embracing the journey, the forge and the flames,
A tapestry woven with hope's vibrant names.

Each ember a story, each spark a new dream,
In the depths of the darkness, life flows like a stream.
The forged forge of belief, where souls intertwine,
In the dance of creation, our hearts brightly shine.

So gather the strength from the fires of old,
Let the flames of our passion in unity behold.
For in the forged forge, our legacy lies,
Together we rise, echoing in the skies.

The Fragmented Heart's Anthem

In shadows deep, where silence dwells,
The heart cries out, where hope compels.
Each shard of pain, a story told,
In whispers soft, the soul's tenfold.

In light's embrace, we seek to mend,
With every prayer, the heavens bend.
Fragments gleam, like stars at night,
Guiding us to eternal light.

Through trials fierce, our faith is tried,
In every tear, our love won't hide.
With shattered dreams, we rise anew,
United strong, our hearts break through.

For in the cracks, His mercy flows,
A healing balm for all our woes.
With every beat, the Anthem sings,
Of grace that life eternal brings.

Grace Upon the Fractured

Amidst the ruins, grace descends,
Each fractured soul, a love transcends.
In valleys low, where shadows creep,
The light of hope, our hearts shall keep.

Through burdens borne, we learn to trust,
In every sorrow, rise from dust.
With open hands, we seek the way,
To find His light in every day.

For grace abounds, though spirits weary,
In whispered prayers, our souls grow cheery.
The fractured paths lead to the whole,
In unity, we heal the soul.

With every step, forgiveness grows,
From bitter roots, compassion throws.
In love's embrace, we find our place,
In fractured hearts, we see His grace.

Sacred Echoes of the Unseen

In quiet stillness, echoes roar,
From depths within, our spirits soar.
Each whispered prayer, a soft refrain,
In sacred trust, we break the chain.

The unseen hands that guide our way,
In every night, we seek the day.
With longing hearts, we stretch and reach,
In silence, love's own truth we teach.

For sacred paths, though often veiled,
In faith we walk, our fears curtailed.
Through darkest nights, the dawn will rise,
In every shadow, His light defies.

In echoes pure, we find our song,
Together bound, where we belong.
With every note, our spirits free,
In sacred echoes, we will see.

Testament of the Torn

In broken fragments, wisdom lies,
The testament of love that tries.
Each scar a mark of battles fought,
In every loss, the peace we've sought.

With heavy hearts, we walk the line,
In cracked foundations, spirits shine.
Each tear a witness to our grace,
A testament of hope we trace.

Though torn and tattered, we remain,
In all the struggles, there’s no shame.
The strength to rise from ashes low,
In every heart, the truth will grow.

For love will weave through every strife,
In brokenness, we find our life.
Together strong, we voice the song,
This testament where we belong.

Flames of Unquenchable Hope

In darkness deep, a light does gleam,
A flicker bright, a holy beam.
With every breath, our spirits rise,
As faith ignites beneath the skies.

Though trials come and shadows fight,
We hold our hearts to warmth and light.
The flames of hope, they dance and sway,
A guiding star to pave the way.

From ashes past, new dreams reborn,
In every heart, a hope to mourn.
With steadfast trust, we face each day,
Holding to love, come what may.

The whispers sweet of angels near,
Their gentle presence calms our fear.
In sacred space, together we stand,
United in faith, hand in hand.

Through stormy seas and restless nights,
The fire within ignites our sights.
With unyielding strength, we dare to cope,
Fueled by flames of unquenchable hope.

Roots of Steadfastness

In soil rich, our spirits grow,
Nurtured deep where rivers flow.
The roots of faith, they stretch and twine,
Anchored strong, a sacred sign.

When tempests roar and shadows loom,
We find our strength amid the gloom.
With every storm, we stand our ground,
In steadfast love, our hope is found.

Through trials faced and burdens borne,
Our hearts are knit, and thus we're sworn.
Like ancient oaks, in grace we rise,
A testament to faith that never dies.

With prayerful hearts, we find our peace,
From worldly chaos, sweet release.
The roots of steadfastness run deep,
In faith we walk, our vows we keep.

In times of strife, we gather near,
Bound by the love that conquers fear.
Together strong, we face each day,
In roots of steadfastness, we stay.

Lanterns in the Storm

When thunder rolls and skies grow gray,
Our hearts will guide, show us the way.
Like lanterns bright, we lift our light,
In darkest nights, we shine so bright.

Through howling winds and heavy rain,
Together we shall bear the pain.
With every flicker, every flame,
We stand as one, in love's great name.

The shadows dance, but fear takes flight,
With faith as fuel, we chase the night.
Our lanterns glow, a sign divine,
In unity, our souls entwine.

As storms may lash and tempests roar,
We rise above, our spirits soar.
For in the darkest, roughest seas,
Our lanterns' light will grant us ease.

With hearts ablaze, we brave the strife,
Embracing hope, the gift of life.
In every soul, a candle's spark,
A beacon bright, to light the dark.

Bridges Over Troubled Waters

When rivers rage and waters churn,
We build our bridges, love to learn.
With hearts united, hand in hand,
We cross the storms, a faithful band.

Through valleys deep and mountains high,
With every step, we will not cry.
For faith is strong, our bond is tight,
Guided by grace, we find the light.

In troubled times, we stand as one,
With courage strong, our fears undone.
The path we tread, though fraught with trials,
Is filled with hope that blesses smiles.

With every bridge, we dare to dream,
As harmony flows like a gentle stream.
Together we rise, a sacred choir,
In love's embrace, we lift each other higher.

Through every wave, we will not yield,
In faith and trust, our hearts revealed.
Creating pathways over storms and strife,
We find our peace, we claim our life.

Pillars of Serenity

In the quiet dawn, grace unfolds,
With whispers of peace, the heart beholds.
Faith like a river, flowing so clear,
In moments of stillness, God draws near.

Each challenge a step, each trial a stone,
In shadows of doubt, our spirits have grown.
Guided by love, we walk hand in hand,
Pillars of hope, together we stand.

The sun gently rises, dispelling the night,
With every soft breath, we draw in the light.
In the strength of our trust, we find harmony,
Serenity blooms, a sacred symphony.

Through valleys of sorrow, the soul learns to sing,
In the arms of the Divine, we find everything.
With gratitude nestled deep in our cores,
The pillars we build open heaven's doors.

As time marches on, let peace be our guide,
With every heartbeat, let love abide.
United in faith, through storms we will sway,
Together forever, in His light, we stay.

Light from Broken Vessels

In shards of our stories, the light starts to gleam,
From fractures and scars, we birth a new dream.
God's grace pours through, even in our pain,
For brokenness brings forth a heavenly gain.

Dust to dust, yet the spirit takes flight,
Through shadows of doubt, we find our true sight.
Each fragment a whisper, a lesson to learn,
In the light of His love, our hearts brightly burn.

From vessels once shattered, we rise and we stand,
Reflections of hope, held in God's hand.
Every tear that we shed waters the ground,
Transforming our hearts, where grace can be found.

With courage as armor, we navigate night,
In unity woven, our souls are alight.
For every broken heart shall be made whole,
A testament forged, the essence of soul.

Let the light illuminate paths that are trod,
In the beauty of brokenness, we meet God.
From shadows emerges a shimmering grace,
In vessels once shattered, love finds its place.

Grains of Unyielding Spirit

In the fields of our lives, we sow and we reap,
With the grains of our trials, harvest runs deep.
Each struggle a seed, sprouting lessons anew,
In the soil of faith, our spirits break through.

With every breath taken, resilience we find,
Like roots that grow strong, intertwined and aligned.
Through tempests that rage, we weather the storm,
In unity's embrace, our spirits transform.

The sun warms our hearts, while shadows may play,
With courage igniting, we brighten the way.
For in suffering's clutch, hope's promise remains,
Grains of unyielding, our joy never wanes.

Through valleys of struggle, we journey with grace,
Finding strength in our numbers, we embrace what we face.
With each step we take, the path becomes clear,
The grains of our spirit, entwined with no fear.

Together we rise, our voices in tune,
As we dance with the stars, and embrace the full moon.
In faith we are anchored, unwavering, bold,
Grains of unyielding spirit, our story unfolds.

Mosaics of Grace

In pieces we gather, each story unique,
A tapestry woven, in hope we seek.
With colors of kindness, our hearts intertwine,
Creating the mosaics, with love we design.

Through trials and triumphs, we fashion our art,
Embracing the fractures, they play their part.
In radiant fragments, our spirits will thrive,
Mosaics of grace, where our dreams come alive.

Shimmering moments, reflecting the light,
In the darkest of places, we shine ever bright.
Each piece tells a tale, of laughter and tears,
In the journey of life, love conquers our fears.

With hands open wide, we welcome the change,
Gathering the shards, as we rearrange.
In the dance of our stories, together we find,
Mosaics of grace, in heartbeats aligned.

As artists of faith, we create without end,
In a world so fractured, we learn to mend.
Let us cherish the beauty, imperfect yet pure,
For in every mosaic, His love will endure.

Footprints in the Valley of Trials

In shadows deep where doubts may creep,
I walk with grace, my soul to keep.
Each step I take on this rugged road,
Your light, O Lord, will ease the load.

Through valleys low, my heart will sing,
Of promises that trials bring.
With every tear that falls like rain,
Your love redeems the deepest pain.

The path may twist, the storm may rage,
Yet in my heart, I'll turn the page.
For in the dark, a promise glows,
In every trial, Your faith still grows.

You guide my feet on weary trails,
Through every storm, as hope prevails.
In Footprints left in dust and stone,
Your presence felt, I'm never alone.

So onward through this vale I stride,
With faith in You, my constant guide.
Though trials loom and shadows play,
Your love will light my darkest day.

Songs of the Unbroken

In times of strife, I'll lift my voice,
For in Your love, I still rejoice.
Unbroken spirit, strong and free,
With every breath, I sing of Thee.

The world may shake, and dreams may fade,
Yet in Your arms, I'm not afraid.
For You, O Lord, will not forsake,
In every trial, my heart won't break.

Through valleys low and mountains high,
I'll raise my song, I'll praise on high.
For every wound, Your balm will heal,
In every struggle, Your love is real.

The chorus rings, the echo strong,
In unity, we join this song.
With hearts entwined in sacred grace,
In every note, we find our place.

So sing, my soul, with joy unbound,
In faith and love, our hope is found.
For songs of the unbroken soar,
In Your embrace, forevermore.

Chariots of Faith’s Journey

In chariots bright, my faith does ride,
Through storms and trials, You’re my guide.
With courage strong, I face the storm,
For in Your love, my soul is warm.

The path ahead may twist and turn,
Yet in my heart, Your light will burn.
Each mile I travel, hand in hand,
With faith as firm as shifting sand.

With chariots soaring, I’ll ascend,
On wings of grace that never end.
For every challenge makes me whole,
In every struggle, I find my soul.

Through trials fierce, I’ll bear Your name,
With every step, my heart aflame.
For faith’s journey is never done,
With You beside me, I have won.

So let the chariots take their flight,
Into the dawn of endless light.
For in this ride, I trust and see,
That every journey leads to Thee.

Windows of Divine Assurance

Through windows wide, Your love shines bright,
A guiding star in darkest night.
With every glance, I find my peace,
In Your embrace, my fears release.

The world outside may roar and clash,
Yet in Your light, I feel the dash.
With hope aflame, my spirit soars,
In windows of grace, my heart restores.

Each moment held in love's embrace,
Creates a path, a sacred space.
For in Your presence, I am whole,
With every breath, You fill my soul.

So through these windows, I shall see,
The beauty of Your love for me.
Each ray of light, a promise clear,
In every moment, You are near.

With faith unwavering, I shall stand,
In windows wide, I lift my hands.
For in Your grace, I find my way,
In every night, there comes the day.

Starlit Paths of Perseverance

Through darkness we walk, guided by light,
Each step we take, a beacon in night.
With faith in our hearts, we journey afar,
The starlit paths shine, our hopes like a star.

Storms may assail, yet we shall not yield,
For strength lies within, the spirit our shield.
In trials we find, a purpose divine,
A tapestry woven, with threads so fine.

The whispers of hope, like soft gentle rains,
Nurturing dreams, erasing our pains.
With every heartbeat, a promise we keep,
To rise from the ashes, our spirits to leap.

In silence we gather, the wisdom of years,
Embracing each moment, through joy and through tears.
A symphony crafted by hands of the wise,
Our lives sing of glory, as time softly flies.

So let us be brave, with courage so vast,
For the starlit paths, hold treasures to last.
In unity's arm, together we stand,
With love as our guide, we shall heal this land.

Guardians of the Heart

In shadows we dwell, yet light does abide,
Guardians surround us, not leaving our side.
With whispers of solace, they echo our fears,
Turning to hope, as they dry all our tears.

Through trials and storms, they strengthen our will,
In moments of doubt, their purpose to fill.
With compassion and grace, they guide us along,
A choir of angels, in symphony strong.

Their presence a balm, in sorrows they mend,
With hearts open wide, they teach us to bend.
In unity's bond, we find our true art,
A tapestry woven by guardians' heart.

In the stillness of night, their voices will call,
Reminding us softly, we're never too small.
For love's gentle touch reaches far and so deep,
Awakening strength in the dreams that we keep.

So trust in their wings, let your spirit take flight,
For together we shine, a beacon of light.
Guardians of heart, in reverence we stand,
Bound by the grace of a divine, loving hand.

Moments of Sacred Fortitude

In the quiet of dawn, hope's whisper begins,
Moments of courage, where true life begins.
Each heartbeat a promise, a vow to the soul,
In sacred fortitude, we find ourselves whole.

Life's path may be steep, with mountains so tall,
Yet within lies the strength to rise from the fall.
Through valleys of despair, we seek the divine,
Holding onto faith, a light that will shine.

With every soft breath, we gather our grace,
In the dance of the brave, we find our place.
For moments of struggle, teach lessons profound,
A journey of love, where wisdom is found.

Stand strong in the face of what bears down on thee,
For trials will pass, like leaves on a tree.
In sacred moments, we ignite our flame,
A testament woven with spirit's own name.

So cherish these moments, hold them so dear,
For each step we take, banishes fear.
In sacred fortitude, let hearts intertwine,
Together we rise, in grace we define.

Wings of Unseen Strength

In silence they soar, with wings made of dreams,
Unseen strength carries, like soft gentle streams.
Through storms they will guide, though hidden from sight,

Leading us onward, through darkness to light.

Each trial we face, a lesson designed,
Wings of unseen strength, our spirits aligned.
With faith as our anchor, we weather the day,
Embracing the journey, come what may.

In whispers of courage, we hear the call,
To rise from our fears, to stand ever tall.
Like eagles in flight, we embrace the unknown,
With wings of resilience, our spirits have grown.

The power within, a force so sublime,
Unseen yet present, transcending through time.
With love as our fabric, our hearts intertwine,
In wings of strength, we shall always shine.

So trust in the journey, and let spirits soar,
With wings of unseen strength, we are forevermore.
For in every challenge, a blessing we find,
In unity risen, our hearts are aligned.

Unyielding Spirit Amidst Ruin

In shadows deep where silence reigns,
The heart shall rise, embracing pains.
Through trials fierce and storms that blow,
A spirit fierce will never bow.

With faith as light, we shall endure,
Each burden borne, we stand secure.
For in the ashes, hope shall grow,
Unyielding hearts, a mighty glow.

When all seems lost and grief is near,
Unseen, a whisper calms the fear.
In every tear, a lesson learned,
A flame ignites, a passion burned.

The path may twist, the road may bend,
Yet love persists, it will not end.
From darkness springs a brighter day,
A testament, we find our way.

So lift your voice and let it soar,
In unity, our spirits roar.
For though we dwell in ruins bleak,
The strength within will always speak.

Resonance of the Redeemer's Touch

In gentle grace, His hand descends,
A balm of peace, the spirit mends.
With every sigh, a sacred chord,
He leads us home, our hearts restored.

The whispers soft, they call our name,
In darkest nights, His love the flame.
Through valleys low and mountains high,
We find our strength, we soar and fly.

With every step, redemption near,
A symphony, so pure, so clear.
The echoes of a love divine,
In every heart, His light will shine.

With open arms, He welcomes all,
No soul too lost, no spirit small.
In tender moments, grace we find,
The Redeemer's touch, so intertwined.

In union sweet, our voices rise,
A chorus bound for sacred skies.
Together, we embrace the truth,
Resonance of eternal youth.

The Hearth of Hope Within Chaos

Amidst the storm, a warmth remains,
A hearth of hope where love sustains.
In chaos swirls, our hearts can bind,
With open arms, we seek and find.

Through tempest's howl, we stand as one,
In darkest hours, our light begun.
With every breath, we draw the flame,
In unity, we rise, proclaim.

From fractured dreams, new visions soar,
A tapestry of strength in lore.
Though shadows loom and trials weigh,
The hearth of hope lights up the way.

Together, we shall weave the night,
With threads of faith, our souls ignite.
In moments lost, we find the thread,
The promise held, the word once said.

Embers glow in every heart,
A shared resolve, a brand-new start.
So gather near, let love be seen,
Within the chaos, hope's evergreen.

Illuminated by the Scars

In every scar, a story told,
A journey marked in threads of gold.
Through pain and trials, we have grown,
Illuminated, we stand alone.

These lines of life etched on our skin,
A testament of where we've been.
With every wound, a lesson dear,
In vulnerability, we shed our fear.

Embrace the past, let shadows fade,
For strength arises from the frayed.
In fractured light, our truth ignites,
Illuminated by love's true sights.

Together, we shall bear the weight,
With open hearts, we celebrate.
In every mark, the light shines bright,
A beacon found in darkest night.

So let us gather, hand in hand,
Our scars a map of promised land.
In unity, we find our way,
Illuminated, come what may.

Visions of the Unwavering

In stillness, faith takes flight,
A beacon shining through the night.
With open hearts and hands held high,
We seek the truth beyond the sky.

Each prayer a whisper in the air,
Binding souls with tender care.
In unity, our spirits soar,
Embracing love forevermore.

The light that guides our every step,
In holy presence, we are kept.
Through trials faced and storms we meet,
We find our strength, we shall not retreat.

With eyes wide open, visions clear,
In faith, we conquer every fear.
The path laid out, we walk in grace,
Together, we shall find our place.

The unwavering heart shall shine,
In every soul, a divine sign.
Hold fast to hope, let love prevail,
For in our hearts, the truth won't fail.

Embrace of the Unseen

In shadows deep, the spirit speaks,
Through whispered dreams, our solace seeks.
An unseen hand both guides and shields,
In silent grace, our fate it yields.

The heart, a vessel for the light,
In darkness found, our souls unite.
Through trials faced, we learn to trust,
In faith we find our grounding dust.

With every moment, love reveals,
The strength that in our silence heals.
Though veiled from sight, we know it’s there,
The spirit's breath, a gentle air.

In sacred stillness, wisdom flows,
In every sorrow, strength we chose.
The unseen binds us, a golden thread,
In love's embrace, we shall be led.

Through every doubt, the heart must rise,
For in the unseen, truth never lies.
Embracing all with open hands,
In unity, forever stands.

Resounding Echoes of Triumph

A mountain high, we climb as one,
With every step, the battle's won.
The echoes of our voices strong,
In harmony, we sing our song.

Through trials faced, we find our might,
In struggles, we ignite the light.
With hearts ablaze, we forge ahead,
In unity, our spirits fed.

The chains of doubt we break apart,
With courage woven in our heart.
In every challenge, victory calls,
With faith unwavering, grace befalls.

Together, united, we shall stand,
Resounding echoes across the land.
In every trial, the light will shine,
In triumph's truth, our souls align.

With every triumph, hope we share,
A testament to love and care.
Through valleys low and heights we gain,
Echoes resounding, joy's sweet reign.

Chronicles of Enduring Love

In every heartbeat, a story told,
A tapestry of love unfolds.
Through seasons changing, love remains,
In every joy and all the pains.

With open hearts, we write the way,
In laughter bright and shadows gray.
The chronicles of love profound,
In every silence, a sacred sound.

Through precious moments, memories live,
In every glance, we learn to give.
With gentle strength, love will sustain,
Through rainy days and sunshine’s gain.

In storms we find a refuge sweet,
In love’s embrace, our souls complete.
Chronicles bound in faith and trust,
In every breath, we rise from dust.

So let us dance through all our days,
In love’s reflection, we shall praise.
For in our hearts, the truth is clear,
Chronicles of love, forever near.

A Psalm from the Pit

In shadows deep, where sorrows lie,
My heart cries out, O Lord,
Lift my spirit, hear my sigh,
With You, my soul is stored.

The pit is dark, the night is long,
Yet faith, a glimmer bright,
Through trials faced, I find my song,
Your love, my guiding light.

Embrace me now, O hands so true,
Transform this weary plight,
With every tear, renew my view,
In darkness, show me light.

The stones of doubt, I cast away,
On Your promise, I'll stand firm,
Your strength shall guide me day by day,
In faith, I will not squirm.

For in the pit, You dwell with me,
Transforming grief to grace,
I rise anew, my heart is free,
In love, I find my place.

Rebirth in Brokenness

From shattered dreams, the heart must rise,
Through pain, a seed must grow,
In brokenness, I see the ties,
That bind me to the flow.

The ashes fall, but hope ignites,
A flame within the night,
With every tear, a new delight,
In darkness, You are bright.

Each wound I bear, a testament,
Of love that bears the weight,
Through trials faced, my soul is lent,
To You, I owe my fate.

Upon the scars, You weave Your grace,
Transforming all I know,
In your embrace, I find my place,
In You, my spirits flow.

Renew my heart, O Lord divine,
In brokenness, I sing,
Embrace my soul, with love entwine,
In unity, I cling.

Foundations Built on Hope's Ashes

From ashes cold, where dreams lay bare,
Hope rises from the ground,
With steadfast hearts, we learn to care,
In faith, our joy is found.

The walls may crack, with years of time,
Yet strength in love shall grow,
With every climb, a higher rhyme,
In trials, true hearts flow.

We build anew on sacred ground,
Each stone a pledge of trust,
In love's embrace, we are profound,
Through every storm, we must.

Our faith, a beacon in the night,
Guiding us through the maze,
With every step in love's pure light,
We rise beyond the haze.

Let hope's foundation hold us fast,
In unity, we stand,
Through all the trials, unsurpassed,
Together, hand in hand.

The Faithful Traveler's Compass

In every journey, guide my feet,
With You, my path is clear,
From mountain high to valley sweet,
In faith, I hold You near.

Through winding roads and rivers wide,
Your Word, my compass true,
With every turn, I shall abide,
In love, I trust in You.

When tempests rise and shadows fall,
Your light shall lead me on,
Through every storm, I heed Your call,
From dusk 'til break of dawn.

With every step, I journey far,
In trials, You are near,
Your strength, my guide, my shining star,
In faith, I shed my fear.

As I traverse this life's great sea,
Your grace, my steady sail,
In every moment, I am free,
With You, I shall prevail.

Held Together by Faith

In the quiet dawn of grace,
Hope shines brightly in our hearts,
Each whisper of love we embrace,
From His mercy, our journey starts.

Through trials and storms, we stand tall,
Faith binds us like a woven thread,
In unity, we will not fall,
For in His light, we are led.

In sacred moments, we find peace,
Our spirits lifted by His might,
With every burden, sweet release,
Together we bask in His light.

We raise our voices, hearts in prayer,
The bonds of trust, we shall defend,
With love that shows we truly care,
Faith's gentle hand will not bend.

In echoes of hope, we rejoice,
For through His love, we are made whole,
Together, we hear His soft voice,
In faith, we find our destined role.

The Invisible Thread of Trust

In shadows deep, where doubts arise,
Trust is the thread that weaves our way,
With every prayer, we reach the skies,
Invisible yet bright as day.

In silence, we forge a connection,
Hearts entwined in a celestial dance,
Every heartbeat a resurrection,
Guided by faith, we take our chance.

With every step, we dare to believe,
The unseen force that draws us near,
In the web of hope, we weave and cleave,
Embracing joy while facing fear.

In each small choice, faith takes its stand,
Trusting the journey, though unknown,
Together we rise, hand in hand,
In every moment, His love is shown.

Through trials endured, our spirits grow,
Trust is the light that guides our way,
In every heart, a sacred glow,
United in love, come what may.

The Pilgrim's Path of Change

Upon the winding road we tread,
Change whispers softly, calling loud,
With every step, new dreams are fed,
In faith, we walk, unbowed, unbowed.

The sunrise paints our souls anew,
With every dawn, fresh hopes ignite,
Embrace the shift, the journey's due,
Trust in the path, a guiding light.

As mountains rise and valleys fall,
We carry forth our sacred trust,
In every trial, we hear His call,
A promise held, we walk through dust.

In moments of fear, hold on tight,
For change is but a divine embrace,
With hearts united, shining bright,
We find our strength in every place.

So let us travel, hand in hand,
The pilgrim's path, a blessed quest,
Through every shift, we understand,
In love and faith, we truly rest.

Sacred Sorrows

In the depths of our sacred pain,
Hearts heavy with burdens we bear,
Every tear falls, like gentle rain,
A testament of love and care.

Through valleys low and shadows deep,
We seek the light that breaks the night,
In every sorrow, promises keep,
His grace awaits in purest sight.

With every struggle, we grow wise,
Learning in trials to rely,
For in the darkness, hope still lies,
In faith, we find the reason why.

Though sacred sorrows may be near,
A bridge is built with each new dawn,
Together facing each hidden fear,
With love, we rise, not to be drawn.

In every tear, a blessing flows,
A sacred bond that cannot break,
Through every heartache, wisdom grows,
Love's gentle touch, for our souls' sake.

Divine Laughter

In moments still, when shadows fade,
There rings a laughter, sweet and pure,
A joy that can never be swayed,
In love’s embrace, we all endure.

The echo of grace in every heart,
A melody of peace divine,
In laughter shared, we find our part,
With every smile, His light will shine.

Through trials faced, we learn to jest,
Life’s burdens eased by joyful cheer,
In playful moments, we are blessed,
Embracing love as we draw near.

Let laughter rise like morning sun,
In every soul, a spark ignites,
Together, we bask in what’s begun,
For joy in faith, our spirits light.

In divine laughter, we find home,
A sacred bond of hearts aligned,
Through every joy, we’re free to roam,
In love’s embrace, forever kind.

Whispers of Courage

In shadows deep, a light does bloom,
A voice that calls amidst the gloom.
With faith as shield, we stand and rise,
Embraced by strength, we touch the skies.

Each trial faced, a chance to grow,
Through storms of doubt, love's winds do blow.
A whisper soft, but oh so strong,
The heart awaits to sing its song.

In tender hands, we hold our fate,
With courage born from love innate.
Together bound, we journey wide,
Through every tear, the Lord's our guide.

A subtle strength, within ignites,
Through darkest nights, our spirits light.
A sacred fire, we nurture still,
A beacon bright, the whisper's thrill.

So let us walk, in grace, in light,
With courage forged from day to night.
For in each heart, a spark of peace,
In whispers shared, our fears release.

Shards of Divine Will

In quiet moments, truths unfold,
A glimpse of grace, a touch of gold.
The will of God, in every soul,
A guiding force that makes us whole.

Through trials fierce, His light will shine,
Each shard we find, a grace divine.
In unity, our spirits soar,
A tapestry of love we bore.

The hands of fate, they weave and twist,
But in His plan, none can resist.
With every breath, His will we taste,
In every challenge, fear replaced.

Embrace the path, though steep and long,
For in the struggle lies His song.
Each shard we hold reflects His grace,
An echo soft, His warm embrace.

Through shattered dreams, we come to see,
The beauty born of mystery.
Each moment sown with love and skill,
A testament of Divine Will.

In every heart, a whisper clear,
Of faith and hope, we persevere.
For through the light, He guides us still,
Upon the shards of His great will.

Relics of Inner Power

Within our hearts, a treasure lies,
Relics of strength beneath the skies.
With every trial, we come to find,
The power deep, our souls aligned.

In silent prayer, we seek the way,
To unlock gifts that never sway.
Each moment still, a chance to grow,
As wisdom blooms, our spirits flow.

In every heartbeat, echoes of grace,
A sacred dance, a boundless space.
The relics found in love's embrace,
Guide us gently, every place.

So let us rise, in faith we stand,
With inner power, hearts in hand.
Through every storm, we'll learn and teach,
The light of love within our reach.

Relics of truth, in whispers told,
Of courage fierce and hearts so bold.
Through every dawn, new light restored,
The inner power, forever soared.

In unity we find our way,
The strength of love, our guiding ray.
With every step, the path unveiled,
In relics held, our spirits hailed.

Sanctuaries of the Soul

In every heart, a sacred place,
A sanctuary filled with grace.
Where whispers soft bring peace anew,
And love's embrace shines bright and true.

Amidst the noise, we seek the still,
A quiet breath to calm the thrill.
In corners deep, our spirits rest,
In faith's embrace, we are so blessed.

Each prayer a thread, each thought a song,
In unity, we all belong.
These sanctuaries, both firm and bright,
Hold sacred truths, a guiding light.

Through trials faced, we find our peace,
In silent love, the hearts release.
A gentle nudge, the soul's delight,
In whispered dreams, we take our flight.

To cultivate the garden fair,
In sanctuaries, we sow our care.
With every dawn, potential grows,
In timeless love, our spirit knows.

So let us stand, united whole,
In every breath, a sacred role.
For in each soul, a space divine,
The sanctuary where love will shine.

The Strength of a Faithful Heart

In trials faced, a spirit shines,
With trust in grace, our hope aligns.
Faith's gentle whisper guides the way,
Through darkest nights, to break of day.

In fervent prayer, our hearts find peace,
A bond with heaven, love will increase.
Each moment spent in quiet trust,
Transforms our fears, as iron to dust.

When burdens weigh like heavy stones,
Faith lifts the soul, and love atones.
With every step, the path revealed,
A faithful heart, forever healed.

In every doubt, a spark remains,
An inner light that breaks the chains.
The strength of faith, a sheltering keep,
In the faithful heart, our hope runs deep.

So let us sing, with joy and cheer,
For love's pure strength will conquer fear.
In unity, we find our part,
With faith, we build a faithful heart.

Glimmers of Hope in Shadows

In shadows deep, where silence dwells,
Glimmers of hope like faint church bells.
Through trials fierce, we seek the light,
The dawn will come to end the night.

Each tear we shed, a prayer in time,
A cry for grace, both pure and prime.
With every heartbeat, courage grows,
In whispered prayers, God's mercy flows.

Though storms may rage and tempests call,
We stand as one, we will not fall.
The glimmers shine, our guiding star,
With faith renewed, we travel far.

In weary steps, we find our way,
With eyes uplifted, we choose to stay.
For hope's embrace, we'll bravely tread,
In shadows deep, His light is spread.

So hold your head through darkest fears,
The glimmers of hope will dry our tears.
With souls united, we'll push through,
In shadows found, our faith rings true.

The Sanctuary of the Struggler

In whispered woes and silent cries,
A sanctuary where the heart lies.
Here faith blossoms, though worn and frail,
In struggle deep, we will not pale.

Each stone we bear, a test of will,
In sacred trust, our spirits thrill.
Through trials harsh, we find our grace,
In every wound, love’s warm embrace.

As tears are shed, the soul is bare,
In sacred space, we feel God’s care.
The struggle leads to strength reborn,
With every heartache, we are sworn.

So gather close, the weary throng,
Together we sing our hopeful song.
In sanctuary found, we heal,
A bond of love, our hearts reveal.

When darkness calls and shadows creep,
In faith we rise, no more to weep.
The sanctuary of the strugglers' sigh,
Becomes a place where spirits fly.

Watering Seeds of Perseverance

In fertile ground, we plant our dreams,
With faith in heart, and hope that gleams.
Each seed a promise, small yet bright,
In patience sown, they reach for light.

The rain will fall, and storms may rage,
Yet steadfast love will turn the page.
With every trial, our roots go deep,
In nurturing care, our spirits leap.

With hands outstretched, we tend the field,
In every struggle, strength revealed.
Though seasons change, we hold the ground,
With perseverance, hope is found.

So as we water, let kindness flow,
In every heart, let love bestow.
With faith as sun, our spirits rise,
In watering seeds, the heart complies.

And when at last the blooms appear,
We'll celebrate with love and cheer.
For every seed that we have sown,
In perseverance, we have grown.

Milton Keynes UK
Ingram Content Group UK Ltd.
UKHW031320271124
451618UK00007B/186